The Weekend Shaman
... and other New Age Types

by Gerry Maguire
Illustrated by Anne Ward

Thorsons
An Imprint of HarperCollins*Publishers*

This book is dedicated to my dad, Rev. George Thompson

Thorsons
An Imprint of HarperCollins*Publishers*
77–85 Fulham Palace Road,
Hammersmith, London W6 8JB

Published by Thorsons 1997
1 3 5 7 9 10 8 6 4 2

A catalogue record for this book
is available from the British Library

ISBN 0 7225 3574 0

Printed and Bound in Great Britain by
Woolnough Bookbinding, Irthlingborough, Northants

What they've said about Gerry Maguire's previous work...

'Loved it – very funny'
– Sue Townsend, author of the Adrian Mole books

'Great swing and relish'
– Seamus Heaney, Nobel prizewinner for poetry

'Witty and informative'
– *Time Out* magazine

'Definitely worth stocking'
– *The Bookseller*

'Great stuff – I've nicked jokes from it!'
– Ken Campbell, comic genius

'Delightful and refreshing'
– Denise Linn, international New Age author and workshop leader

'…the sort of stuff I could sit on the loo with for hours'
– Simon Bates, sacked Radio One DJ

'I don't know what all the fuss is about'
– Gerry's Mum

The characters depicted in these pages, of course, don't actually exist – they are merely exaggerated caricatures of tendencies that most of us exhibit in one way or another. Hopefully, then, they will enable us to have a good laugh at ourselves – as valuable as any healing.

Irish author Gerry Maguire has written a number of books, both serious and humorous, on personal transformation subjects. He is also a live comedy performer and founder of Positive Comedy Productions.

Gerry is a Buddhist. His spiritual name is Chikkentikkenanda.

Illustrator Anne Ward, also Irish, has worked with Maguire on a number of previous books, including *Astral Sex to Zen Teabags*. As well as book illustration, she works in animation.

The cartoons are the joint work of the author and the illustrator; Maguire provided the concepts, content and words, and Ward prepared the drawings.

Contact details:
Positive Comedy Productions
Brighton Media Centre
11 Jew Street, Brighton
BN1 1UT, UK
Tel + 44 (0)1273 206000/ 563495
Email: gerry@pavilion.co.uk

Contents

The Weekend Shaman

The Weekend Shaman is a steady, serious sort of chap.

During the week, his life is a dull round of meetings, reports, memos, spreadsheets and bar-charts. But at the weekend he suddenly comes alive. He swaps his sharp suit for an authentic Native American outfit of loin-cloth, head-dress, beads and cute buckskin Navajo jacket. He speaks earnestly about the Great Spirit. He drums badly, lacking any sense of rhythm whatsoever. He was disappointed when his Medicine Chief gave him the spirit name 'Dances-with-Attitude'. He regards the bear, wolf and eagle as his totem animals, but gets terrified when he finds a spider in the bath.

One weekend will be spent on an initiation into Shapeshifting for Beginners; the next might be purifying your pet through Hopi smudging techniques, or Celtic Journeying to the Underworld. During annual leave, he will embark on a Vision Quest in the mountains. He will make sure he brings along his four-season sleeping bag, Arctic Storm tent, satellite position indicator, mobile phone, and fat John Grisham novel. He will return to the office feeling spiritually renewed and deeply reconnected to the Sacred. He dreams of one day going to live among indigenous people that still preserve a prehistoric shamanistic culture, perhaps in the wild mountains of Siberia.

There is a female variation of the Weekend Shaman – a more earthy creature altogether. Her spirit name will be something like Mighty Powerful She-wolf or perhaps Loves-to-Eat-Cake. Her favourite shamanistic event is the monthly all-female 'We-Moon' gathering, where sisters get into the creative side of menstruation, sitting together on clumps of moss, nourishing Grandmother Earth and complaining about men.

The Self-appointed Guru

The Self-appointed Guru is an intriguing figure. Perhaps he was once a bricklayer – no-one knows, for everything about his past is shrouded in a cloak of mystery – he retains a team of cover-up agents to keep it that way; together with a huge retinue of other invisible people – financial whizz-kids, beard stylists, jewellery advisers, muesli, spin-doctors, inspiration think-tanks and assorted sycophants. For, as well as being extremely enlightened, he is extremely successful, extremely popular and extremely rich.

His followers hang on his every word; if they cannot find deep significance in his utterances, he urges that they will do when they too reach a more enlightened state. He recommends that they abandon everything to follow him; yet paradoxically he doesn't seem to feel the need to abandon anything himself – rather he seems to acquire things. It's different for him – as he operates on such a superior plane, he's not adversely affected by material possessions, desire or greed. He advises celibacy, but compassionately permits some of his more beautiful female acolytes to sleep with him – purely in the interests of their own spiritual growth, of course. Indeed, the use of paradox seems to be one of his favourite teaching devices. He changes his spiritual name often, perhaps to symbolize his lack of attachment and constant upward shift through levels of consciousness, or maybe just for the hell of it.

You might be tempted to think that anyone could do this job, but you'd be wrong; it takes a very special kind of person. You need incredibly thick skin, extraordinary arrogance, astounding ego, unlimited self-centredness, boundless greed, total lack of conscience or scruples and a talent for keeping smiling whatever happens. Plus a knack for stressing how *ordinary* you are.

The Past Life Junkie

The Past Life Junkie is entirely convinced that everything that happens to her in this life is directly due to something else that occurred in a former incarnation.

She is sure, for instance, that her current back problems are due to the unwelcome attentions of the Spanish Inquisition. Her heat rashes stem from burning at the stake as a Cathar martyr. She's been allergic to stripey cats ever since being mauled by a tiger in colonial India. Her dairy intolerance is traceable to drowning as a young princess in her daily bath of asses milk. She still can't touch wheat, because she was once squashed between granary millstones.

This person has been hung, strangled, suffocated, guillotined, garrotted, shot by firing squad, buried in a pyramid, sacrificed to rain-gods, dismembered by conquistadors, skinned by Jesuits, and assassinated by a younger sister. Oh yes, and smothered in honey, then eaten by termites in the desert. She is terrified of death, simply because she's been killed so many times.

And she has many varied and unusual sexual predilections that are obviously past-life related; for she's been an infamous harlot, a royal concubine, a vestal virgin, and the Marquis de Sade's house-keeper; and her past residencies include both Sodom and Gomorrah. Consequently she really only achieves a satisfactory climax these days in a semi-public situation and when completely covered in chocolate.

Somehow, she seems to accompany the same partner who incarnates with her for lifetime after lifetime, and who is now her husband. And guess what – he was also the younger sister who assassinated her, the Jesuit who skinned her, the conquistador who dismembered her – and the guy who smeared her with honey before turning her over to the termites.

The Celestine Prophet

The Celestine Prophet is a fascinating, enigmatic figure, who leads an intriguing double life. Officially, he's a nice regular-guy kind of therapist, quietly minding his own business in a sleepy backwater in the Deep South of the USA. But in the other half of his Jekyll-and-Hyde existence he is a jet-setting New Age Indiana Jones type, who secretly takes off on a high adventure among the rainforest and lost cities of the Peruvian mountains – engaged in life-and-death pursuits by the military and church authorities, while searching for photocopies of 9,000-year-old manuscripts, which contain insights that reveal the universal truths of life, and unravel the mysteries of the universe itself. After he succeeds on this mission of destiny – chiefly by going with the flow and not doing very much of anything – he returns to his sleepy backwater, and self-publishes his adventure as a metaphysical thriller which becomes an instant cult hit and worldwide bestseller. Nobody knows whether it's true or not, so it gets to the top of both fiction and non-fiction lists.

His cover is now well and truly blown. The material goes on to generate a spin-off industry that includes more books, videos, courses, tee-shirts and further insights. So now everyone in the world possesses these secretive percep-tions, namely: that life consists of a series of meaningful coincidences; that everything is composed of energy, including us; that we should all be nicer to each other, or else something terrible will happen; that we all eventually disap-pear; and that you can't make an omelette without breaking eggs.

So that's all there is to being a Celestine Prophet; it's as simple as that. It could happen to anyone; or so that nice therapist guy from the Deep South would have us believe…

The Malebonder

Male-bonding has been going on since there were males to bond – but it has only really come into its own with the advent of the Men's Movement. The true Malebonder is a child of this wonderful and powerful phenomenon.

On first impressions, he looks just like your average total meat-head macho type, who would throw you into the middle of next week for suggesting that he possessed such a thing as an emotion. But this guy has been transformed. One fine day, he accidentally stumbled into his local men's group, and discovered what he had secretly always craved – a safe space to get in touch with his feelings, own his true vulnerability, and admit that inside this big, tough guy there's always been a tiny, frightened kid who's good at pretending that he's really brave. And he's discovered that all the other guys are the same! He's been to the Robert Bly workshops, and he knows all about Iron John. For him, the term 'men's work' has taken on a whole new meaning.

And so he has got past the mutual suspicion and fear of masculine relating, and set aside the tyranny of male stereotyping; he has learned to treasure instead the common ground he shares with other men. He has let his sexuality out into the open. He has shared with them, one and all, the universal grief from the father's absence, and the anger at the mother for driving the father away. He has re-discovered his gentler, more creative side, and discovered a surprising passion for macramé. He has moved from a culture of male competitiveness and rivalry to one of support and shared intimacy. He has found that big boys do cry, and he spends every free weekend on a big, male cry-fest in the woods. But he's still scared of that hairy man at the bottom of the pond.

The Near-Death-Experiencer

Near Death Experiences do not happen to New Age folks, but to ordinary people. The average recipient is not very spiritual at all – she worries more about her figure, and what's on TV tonight. Then she has her NDE. She drowns, or has a heart attack, or some such terrible accident; there now unfolds a standardized sequence of events. She feels herself floating up out of her body, which she can now see below her; perhaps it is surrounded by a group of people who are still trying to revive her, on the riverbank or roadside or in the hospital operating theatre. She is filled with an incredible sense of wellbeing.

She finds herself far from this scene; she is walking down a long, dark tunnel. Soon she sees light ahead, brighter than anything she has ever seen; she knows that this is the Light of Pure Eternal Love. And as she nears the end of the tunnel she can see a landscape of breathtakingly beautiful fields, filled with trees and flowers, with many happy souls walking together. Her ears are filled with the haunting sound of angelic choirs. Her whole being is suffused with the essence of peace, love and harmony. She yearns to enter this land.

But suddenly she is aware of another sound – the Voice of the Divine – which tells her that she is not yet ready to enter – that she cannot leave the mortal world; she must return to her earthly state and complete important work there, and perhaps watch less TV. So back she must go.

And now her whole outlook on life changes. She becomes an incredibly spiritual person. She spreads joy all round, and does good works. And she never again worries about death, money, cellulite – or eating too much chocolate.

The Tantric Sex Fiend

This man amazes you. By his own accounts, he is the total master of his own sexuality. Apparently he considers seven-hour intercourse to be 'a quickie'. He has developed his sexual muscles to the point where he can use them to pick up a pea. He hasn't ejaculated for 15 years. For his partners, he doesn't count anything under 10 as a multiple orgasm. What he can't tell you about pheromones, kundalini and erogenous zones isn't worth knowing. He can tell the difference between the clitoris, the G-spot and the perineum. He can do semen retention till sexual ecstasy is coming out of his ears.

His bookshelves groan under the weight of unexpurgated volumes of the *Kama Sutra* and *The Perfumed Garden*, of the Hite report, Kinsey, Masters and Johnson, and any in-your-face sex manual that's ever been published. His small talk is full of the quaint, poetic allusions of classical eroticism, all about his 'Piercer' and her 'Jade Room' and 'The Final Transcendence of Passion'. He can go on at great length about every esoteric position, from the relatively straightforward 'Bull among the Cows' to the anatomically impossible 'Flying Ducks Reversed'. His own personal favourite is known as 'The Plumbing Repair Man' (you stay in all day but nobody comes).

But sometimes you wonder about him. He claims that all this stuff is only a sort of incredibly advanced form of meditation – it's not really about sex or pleasure, it's about following the spiritual path towards enlightenment and self-realization. Yeah, right! And, with all this wonderful stuff going on, what a terrific way to get laid. Anyway, if he's so good at it, how come he has to keep finding so many new partners?

The Wounded Healer

The Wounded Healer is a proud character who casts himself in the mould of one of the great archetypes. He follows in the footsteps of Chiron, a centaur figure of classical Greek mythology, who was struck by a poisoned arrow. He suffered from this throughout his whole life, and travelled the world, looking in vain for a cure. But this tireless searching enabled him to develop the ability to heal others, and for this he was finally rewarded by becoming a star of the firmament. Thus came about the archetype of the Wounded Healer. Unfortunately, many healers that have some little thing wrong with them suddenly think fit to identify themselves with this grandly tragic yet heroic figure.

Modern Wounded Healers seem to go one of two ways in how they relate to their own condition. They either acknowledge their woundedness and wallow in it, or they go into total denial. The self-confessedly wounded ones are sad cases, but there is hope for them; they may yet make progress, learn something from the process and apply it to the benefit of others.

The second type is much more worrying. This variation is known as the Unhealed Healer – the one who's totally obsessed with helping other people, leaving their own healing processes and their unresolved personal issues completely untouched. Tell-tale signs of this condition are: addiction to doing healing; trying to heal people in inappropriate circumstances; not being able to relate to people other than through healing them; wanting to heal people who have nothing wrong with them; being angry, tense, depressed and hyperactive; and draining people around them of their vital energy in auric-vampire style. These are clearly the last people you'd want to go to for help in getting yourself sorted out. Still, nobody's perfect.

The Colonic Irrigationist

You enter the room nervously, for this is your first session, and you're not sure what to expect. Your apprehension is exacerbated when you find that the Colonic Irrigationist is extremely attractive, with an exuberant personality and an earthy sense of humour; she clearly enjoys her work. It's all very straightforward, she explains enthusiastically; a sterile speculum is placed in your rectum; water is pumped in and then out again, cleansing the bowel thoroughly of toxic waste matter that may have been lining its walls for some considerable time. You may find it quite a pleasant sensation. And you'd probably be interested to monitor the results as they pass through the viewing tank, over there. And yes, it's a little too late to change your mind…

Colonic Hydrotherapy, as it is euphemistically called, was for decades favoured only by the oddest aficionados of bodily puritanism – the kind of people who like nothing better than to fortify themselves each day with a large glass of urine. In recent years, however, it was suddenly embraced as the pleasure of the rich, famous and royal. Since then, it seems to have moved on downmarket and become the therapy of choice for the most unexpected of clienteles; great macho footballers, who once feared nothing more than the thought of a foreign body entering their lower intestinal tract, are lining up for it in droves.

One does tend to wonder, though, about the motives of those who opt for this particular method of earning a living, for it isn't everyone's cup of tea. To ply this trade, you need a strong stomach, a steady hand, nerves of steel, and a natural ability to deal with the hazards of anal retentiveness.

It's dirty work, as they say, but somebody's got to do it. And by the way – please don't try this at home.

The X Files Obsessive

This young fellow lives, breathes, eats and sleeps the *X Files*. He has never missed an episode or repeat, even though he has them all on video. He goes to all the fan conferences. He possesses every spin-off item that the series has ever generated. He worries his parents sick with the amount of time he spends on-line, discussing with other fanatics everything about Duchovny and Anderson, from who they're dating and whether they will ever get married to each other, to what pets they keep and what's been found this week in their garbage. His favourite episode is the one about this wolfman who's been raised by mutant cockroaches and lives under the New York subway system, and is now manifesting some serious anti-social behaviour so it's time to call in Fox Mulder and Dana Scully.

And the X Files Obsessive believes it all. It doesn't concern him that their relationship is pure, calculated chemistry and unresolved sexual tension. It doesn't bother him that all the evidence they ever uncover is always wiped out by some sinister government agent by the end of each show, and they're always back to square one at the start of the next one, so that the series can go on for ever. It doesn't seem odd to him that these two always appear in such nice stylish clothes, no matter how disgusting their mission, or that they have never had a bad-hair day however extreme the violence they are subjected to. And it hasn't occurred to him that in each episode something weird happens, Mulder thinks it's the work of aliens or something paranormal, Scully thinks there's a perfectly natural scientific explanation, then it turns out that Mulder was right and it was *extremely* paranormal, and then the same thing happens the next week and every other week, yet Ms Scully never seems to catch on that maybe she should look at things a bit differently.

The Feng Shui Apprentice

Feng Shui can change your life – your health, your relationships, your success, your bank balance; and nobody knows this better than the Feng Shui Apprentice. He may only have attended a couple of weekend workshops, but he is already doing brisk business. Lacking any serious qualifications, he calls his work Intuitive Feng Shui.

He does, however, have a good command of the terminology. He knows how to pronounce the name of his art correctly ('Fung Shway'). He can use the word 'energy' in many different ways – the flow of energies, the clearing of stuck energies, the deflection of disharmonious energies, the enhancement of positive energies … And he never goes anywhere without his Bagua compass, not even on a picnic. He cultivates something of an oriental manner – bowing a lot, pronouncing his Rs badly, sleeping at night with sticky tape over his eyes to produce the inscrutable look of someone that can see beneath the surface of things.

He can easily convince you that all that happens in your life is due to the arrangement of stuff in your home. Traditional housewives in particular fall prey to this – they have always felt that they could change their lives by rearranging the furniture, or painting the bathroom a different colour. He likes surprising people with his esoteric recommendations. He declares that moving an ornament on your mantelpiece a little to the left will stop your marriage falling apart. He recommends that you place your desk in the bathroom. He says you must put food out at night because you have Hungry Ghosts.

If you've done what he says, yet found that your problems have got worse rather than better, don't bother coming looking for him. By then, he'll have given up on Feng Shui and become a Reiki Master.

The Flaky Reiki Master

The Flaky Reiki Master is one of the brightest rising stars in the galaxy of new-found therapies. Reiki (pronounced 'ray-key') activates one's cosmic life energies.

Now, the word 'master' used to mean that you had to spend about 50 years doing something; thankfully, those days are now over. You can learn Reiki very quickly; each stage or 'degree' can be acquired in a weekend. For it is simply a direct transmission from one person to another; you just become an instant master. There's only the question of cost, for the fees for these transmissions are rather high. But don't worry, because you can go straight out on the following Monday morning and set up workshops to initiate others. What a terrific concept!

This is why the Reiki world is characterized by ever-spiralling initiation fees and numbers of people getting in on the act. Consequently there are less clients available, and so the only viable option is to focus on training others. At the current rate of increase, everyone in the Northern hemisphere will be a Reiki Master by the year 2005 – but without any clients. So something will have to change.

And it *is* changing. Some charlatans are beginning to spoil it for everyone else, by offering cut-price Mastery, and giving deals like 'Pay for two degrees and get the third one free!' But the Reiki mandarins have a simple strategy for fighting this – inventing new Reiki degrees. Once there were only three, then there were seven, and there is nothing to stop the number rising. And of course, the new levels will naturally be more expensive than ever…

Thus the star of Flaky Reikidom is set to shine brighter than ever. It remains to be seen, though, whether it goes on to create a whole new galaxy of its own – or suddenly implodes into a great big Black Hole.

The Sloppy Astrologer

Everyone knows at least one of these guys. He's highly critical of horoscopes that are printed in popular newspapers and magazines; they're shallow, formulaic and exploitative. *His* work is quite different. He contributes to your process of personal transformation, and promotes your emotional development. It's all about new beginnings, dynamic breakthroughs and intense realizations. It's about the profoundest aspects of your spiritual life journey.

He is full of technical-sounding terms like quincunx and sextile. He drops convincing remarks about your aspects and transits and Saturn Returns. He casually mentions the influence of planets, like Chiron or Ophiucus. He tells you what you wish to hear, but is never too specific about it. He sticks to predictions that have a better than 50:50 chance of happening. He remarks that you may receive some excellent news in the coming months, rather than saying that you're going to be promoted at work next week. He incorporates a fair number of contradictory predictions, to be on the safe side.

When you get home, you're hard pushed to pin down a single tangible thing that he said. He covers up for his lack of hard astrological skills by emphasizing that he works at a very instinctive and spiritual level – or, as we would say, he makes it up as he goes along. At parties, he is often able to 'intuit' people's sun-signs, because he has earlier taken the trouble to discover their birth dates.

Actually, what this man does is an airy-fairy version of the popular horoscopes that he scorns. And in a month or so he might have abandoned astrology and taken up freelance journalism; but then that's probably because he's an Aries…

The Motivational Trainer

The Motivational Trainer is a little hard to believe at first. He is strikingly tall, stunningly handsome, exceptionally articulate and extremely charismatic. He's incredibly dynamic, supremely confident, unbelievably successful and absurdly wealthy. And he feels okay about all of this. *And* he's a genuinely nice guy. This really cuts across our ideas of what is possible in a human being – which is exactly what he wants it to do.

His achievements are certainly no mean feat. His presentations bring together the insights of personal empowerment, the wisdom of ancient religion, the PR of politicians, the business skills of top salesmanship, and the stage management of a rock star. His audiences stretch away as far as the eye can see, and each member of it is under his spell. His every word is carefully chosen, tried and tested. Each gesture is carefully researched and honed to perfection.

And he certainly delivers the goods. He brings you the seminar, the book, the video, the transformational assault course. He supplies you with the techniques, the strategies, the mission statements. He shows you how to get the maximum results in the minimum time. He convinces you that you too can take control of your life, change your self-limiting perceptions, get rid of your negative beliefs, discover your true purpose, harness the forces that control your destiny, and achieve your peak performance. You too can fill your life with unlimited power. You too can be incredibly rich, successful, handsome and happy. And it's just as well that the Motivational Trainer *is* incredibly rich, successful, handsome and happy, because if he wasn't then we wouldn't believe it worked, would we?

The Sadistic Acupuncturist

Acupuncture is excellent for all kinds of pain – causing it, that is. Acupuncturists don't call their work 'needling' for nothing.

The Sadistic Acupuncturist has an unerring way of homing in on your most vulnerable points – you could say that her instinct for it is needle sharp. But her strategies are subtle; she doesn't lay it too heavily on you at first, and this is why many people notice that their treatments hurt a little more each time. At first she will place the needles in quite reasonable places like your back or the fleshy bits of your arms and legs. After a couple of sessions, she'll move to more sensitive areas such as your buttocks, abdomen, and ears. When you can tolerate this, she'll move on to your fingertips, lips and maybe the inside of your nose. And if you don't stop seeing her at this point she'll suddenly find it imperative to treat your tongue, genitals or eyeballs.

She also has a battery of techniques that help refine the torture. After she initially sticks a needle into you, she might wiggle it about or push it in further. She can attach blocks of burning herbs to the tops of the needles, or wire them up to electricity to jolt you out of any composure you may have left. Before starting she might have said that you may feel 'a slight tingling'. This is rather like getting an elephant to sit on someone and telling them that they might detect a slight tickling sensation. Throughout the session, she will remain impassive to your suffering; this is enabled by the oriental inscrutability she has learned during her training in China.

Oh well, at least she offers an effective possibility for disciplining horrid New Age children: 'If you don't behave, I'm going to send you to the acupuncturist!'

The Self-centred Counsellor

There are many different kinds of counselling, which may be loosely grouped according to their focus. There's client-oriented counselling, group-oriented counselling, and process-oriented counselling; but the one you really want to avoid is counsellor-oriented counselling.

There is no question that it can be a terrible burden for one human being to take on the weight of another's sufferings and personal tragedies; and the Self-centred Counsellor's clients can become keenly aware of this burden. It's not that he hasn't been in therapy himself – he's had Freudian Analysis, Post-Freudian Analysis, and Analysis to undo the adverse effects of Freudian Analysis. Perhaps he's like this because he was consistently ignored by his father as a child, or maybe his mother only breast-fed him once. Perhaps he's opted into being a therapist so that he can extract this bizarre form of revenge on the human race. He emphasizes that counselling is a process of give and take – he takes, and the client gives.

There are certain warning signs that may alert you to this tendency in a therapist. Perhaps you will notice him peppering the conversation with remarks like, 'I've felt like that too, sometimes', or making very long interjections that begin, 'What I hear you saying is … ' Perhaps you'll notice that he stares out of the window a lot. Maybe you arrive for a session, and discover that he's gone to the movies on the spur of the moment.

The one thing that the Self-centred Counsellor is really good at is helping you get in touch with your suppressed anger, and let you discover that you have an unexpected capacity for the unsolicited Primal Scream. In fact, he has a broken nose to prove his skill in this department.

The Extreme Sports Freak

The Extreme Sports Freak is not so much an endangered species as a species that loves danger. The thrill, the buzz, the adrenaline rush – these are what he seeks; it's all about avoiding boredom – and looking really cool.

Extreme sports have always been a youth-culture thing. It started in the 60s, in trendsetting locales like California and Colorado. Sports such as surfing, skiing and mountain climbing were obviously far too boring and far too safe, so dangerous variations were evolved – free climbing, sky-surfing, shark-punching, and water-skiing without skis. Having your spine in good shape was very dull so bungee-jumping arrived. Soon the Extreme Sports Freak finds himself white-water rafting without the raft, climbing the Matterhorn with his hands tied behind his back, or joining a team parachute jump where one person gets a dummy 'chute bag on his back. At least he won't be bored.

None of this activity is any good if it isn't seen. Extreme Sports are essentially spectator sports, and there are usually plenty of spectators; not only fellow-maniacs but also guys whose personal idea of extreme danger is dating a feminist or maybe roller-blading in the park on a Sunday afternoon.

The Extreme Sports Freak, of course, displays all the teenager's rebellious disdain while still lapping up the attention, and cultivating the exclusive lingo. There he was, for instance, *boning it out* and really *shredding fakie* on a terrific *stiffy* till some *pinhead eurocarved* him and he was *wiped out*, doing a *face-plant* in the *crud*. But he still managed to get in a *stale fish*, a *chicken wing* and some *Canadian bacon*. So in the end it was truly *gnarly*.

Most girls have too much common sense and self-preservation instinct for all this. You do find the occasional *shred betty*, though…

The Sham Vegetarian

This person is very principled – she's a vegetarian in principle, but not in practice.

You've heard of the lacto-vegetarian, who also eats dairy products, and the lacto-ovo-vegetarian, who takes dairy and eggs too; well, this woman just happens to be a lacto-ovo-carno-vegetarian. But she doesn't eat meat indiscriminately – only on certain occasions; like when invited out to a restaurant that doesn't have a vegetarian menu, or when the meat course looks more delicious, or the willpower just isn't there. Or, let's face it, simply when nobody's looking. But people will know anyway – the Sham Vegetarian can easily be distinguished from the real thing because she doesn't have the authentic gaunt look, the austere manner, the teeth worn down by grit and stones that lurk among the grains and pulses, and the obsessive need to know the ingredients in everything. Perhaps a better name for her would be Opportunistic Vegetarian – one who eats meat when the opportunity arises.

She has a battery of excuses ready for those who question her ethical stance – 'I can't tell my mom I'm vegetarian; she might have a heart attack'; 'I'm *mainly* vegetarian'; 'My dietician said I needed it'; 'I never eat red meat'; 'Chicken isn't really meat'; 'It's not a moral thing, anyway – it's a health thing'; and 'I only eat happy, organic meat' – as if the most idyllically-reared bio-dynamic sheep is going to remain euphoric when about to get the chop.

And so she goes on having the best of both worlds – eating a totally pumpkin-based feast on the winter solstice, and then digging into turkey with all the trimmings at Thanksgiving or Christmas. After all, to do anything else would be denial – and that wouldn't be right, would it?

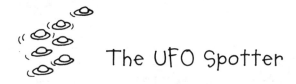

The UFO Spotter

The Ufologist is fascinated by those beings who, for reasons best known to themselves, visit our planet to make crop circles, abduct human beings, keep us guessing about how intelligent they are, and have their flying objects remain unidentified.

The UFO Spotter is extremely upset at how the whole issue of UFOs was first marginalized, then ridiculed, and now sensationalized by the mainstream media and public opinion. He reckons the truth is that about 75 per cent of people in the world have seen a UFO, and that 15 per cent have been abducted at one time or another. He's not at all traumatized by his own personal experiences of abduction, which of course is nothing at all to do with the drugs he was on at the time.

Other people believe in aliens and UFOs, but consider their motives to be much more sinister – they're just waiting for the moment to attack us in vast numbers. After all, the word 'Extraterrestrial' implies someone who wants more land, doesn't it? Others think that they have lost their physiological technology to reproduce themselves, and are hoping to recover the ability by tinkering with the reproductive organs of abductees; yet others are sure that since ancient times alien entities have been occupying the bodies of earthlings as 'walk-ins'. A smaller group has a theory that they only stop off at the planet Earth when they happen to be passing nearby on a major interstellar voyage, and just need to do whatever is their equivalent of taking a leak; and that this activity somehow involves lots of flashing lights and trampling of corn. Who knows – perhaps *they're* right.

The Conspiracy Theorist

As a child, this chap was convinced that his mother was always keeping some really special food hidden away from him. As a teenager, he was sure that all his high-school friends were getting sex when he wasn't. And as an adult, he has discovered that far more worrying things are being hidden from him – and from the rest of humanity.

He now knows, for instance, that Marilyn Monroe didn't commit suicide, that the CIA got rid of John Kennedy, that the moon landing was filmed in a TV studio and that aliens have been to the White House for afternoon tea.

Furthermore, he knows that all such conspiracies are co-ordinated by something called the Military-Industrial Complex, a confederation of all the world's armies, governments, secret police, media and international corporations. In fact, world affairs are orchestrated by a group of seven powerful Swiss gnomes who live in a suburban garden in Zurich. And he's just found out that, many millennia ago, a group of interstellar entities usurped control of the planet Earth, diverting it to serve their own evil purpose by rearranging our DNA.

But it's not just unsavoury information that is being covered up, he realizes. The MIC is suppressing all kinds of inventions that would make life better for many millions of people like simple devices for creating energy out of nothing, for making grass edible by humans, and for converting politicians into honest people. Clearly, none of these are going to see the light of day. But perhaps his most worrying realization is that the discovery of all these conspiracies may in fact be a highly elaborate construct that has been meticulously planted by 'Them' to distract attention from something much more sinister…

The Obnoxious Aromatherapist

Aromatherapy is a smelly and expensive business, involving the use of essential oils massaged into the skin in a carrier such as almond oil.

The Obnoxious Aromatherapist takes this a bit further. Her home is a world of overwhelmingly pungent odours; you can't quite be sure which are coming from the essential oils and which from her. Among the smells that you can identify are a strong reek of dear old ladies (Lavender), a whiff of the Orient (YlangYlang), and far too much Patchouli, or Oil of Old Hippie. Your nose is also picking up on something like Eau de Armpit. If you can detect Evening Primrose too, watch out – that means she's got PMT as well.

As she begins the treatment, you are assured that you will soon feel incredibly stimulated, calmed, uplifted and relaxed, all at the same time. Today, she's going to use her favourite aroma – Essence of Viper's Sex-gland. And that economy carrier she's using – surely it can't be Cod Liver Oil? And does she really need to pummel you into a wobbling jelly like this, just to make you feel relaxed?

The surprising thing about the Obnoxious Aromatherapist is that she is petite, yet as strong as an ox. She probably has a background in nursing and cosmetics, and moved over into this area because of the very convenient masking smell.

As the treatment draws to a close, she asks how you feel, and you sense that it wouldn't be wise to report feeling tense and nauseous, with an over-riding urge to get the hell out of there. Nor does it seem the ideal moment to say that she might have a personal hygiene problem. So you ooze rapture, and leave.

And so, to paraphrase the label on many essential oil bottles: This Aromatherapist can cause irritation, and should be used cautiously – if at all.

The Mediocre Medium

This chap is one of the nicest fellows you could hope to meet but somehow he doesn't seem to have his psychic abilities fully under control. While sitting on the bus, for instance, he will inadvertently slump over, enter trance state, and start speaking in a strange voice with an Irish/Transylvanian accent. On several occasions this has led to embarrassing arrest.

There are sometimes moments of lucidity. He once channelled the spirit of Edgar Cayce, but all the great man had to say was that his rheumatism was really bothering him. On another occasion, the Ascended Masters used him to voice complaints that they couldn't get fish and chips wherever it was that they had ascended to. Perhaps his most dramatic visitation was when he endeavoured to channel the widely-loved entity Emanuel, and got instead a long and explicitly erotic episode from the pornographic film star of the same name. This occurred at the peak of his career, in front of an elderly audience of several hundred, who had all left by the time he came to.

Nowadays, though, his messages are a little more pedestrian, usually involving somebody's grandmother being worried about them, or someone else's cat that has crossed over to the other side. He tried his hand at exorcism, but the ghosts wouldn't take him seriously. And the one time he tried automatic writing, all he got was Cleopatra's shopping list.

His worst problem, though, is undoubtedly the naughty entity called Pandora who nips in when he's in trance at home and uses the phone. This mischievous sprite is particularly fond of calling cabs for him when he isn't going anywhere, ordering pizzas with toppings that he doesn't like, and calling the emergency services to say that his house is on fire.

The Leyline Hunter

The Leyline Hunter is something of a hybrid, incorporating the esotericism of the Earth Mysteries enthusiast, the practicality of the metal detector user, and the burning passion of the train spotter. Thus equipped, he dowses the country high and low for the lines of low-frequency electro-magnetic energy that criss-cross the earth.

These fascinating lines, he will point out to you enthusiastically over a pint of real ale in the Avebury Arms pub, link together ancient sacred sites, in absolutely straight lines, all over the world. In Britain alone, he continues eagerly, these deeply significant meridians were familiar to the Neolithic settlers, Celts, Pagans, Romans, Saxons, Normans, medieval church builders, and his own great-grandfather who wrote a booklet on the subject in 1841. In fact, he goes on emphatically, all megalithic monuments are located on ley centres, where leylines cross – they're known as power points, as if the earth has a big electrical wiring system, and the monuments are appliances that you plug in to connect to the source. And did you know that these stone circles and dolmens and tumuli were all constructed with incredible awareness of a universal system of sacred geometry. Oh, yes. Or that – really warming to his subject now – archaeologists think they were just places for the Druids to bury a few bodies or sacrifice a couple of unfortunate individuals, but no – they're actually incredibly accurate astronomical devices that give amazingly detailed information about the solstices and the equinoxes and the movement of the planets. And these people had an extremely advanced civilization which…

…And as your attention begins to wander, you do a bit of mental dowsing yourself, and decide it's time to leave.

The Born-again Rebirther

Rebirthing was founded in California in the 1970s by a salesman called Leonard Orr, and has been characterized by the qualities of Californianism and salesmanship ever since.

Mr Orr decided that every last thing about you is due to whatever happened in your birth process. People whose birth was overdue, for instance, will go through life always being late for everything. Those who were born prematurely constantly arrive too early. If your mother had a home birth, you will always be a house-proud sort of person, and not enjoy going out very much. If it was a water-birth, you'll be a terrific swimmer. If she received an epidural, you'll always have an extremely low threshold of pain. If yours was a breech birth you'll be one of those energetic individuals who jumps into everything feet first. If you were induced you will always need to be talked into doing things. If you were in an incubator, you'll always want the central heating turned high. And if you came out with the umbilical cord caught round your neck, you'll be very fond of macramé and creative knotwork; but if you were the product of a Caesarean you'll prefer attacking people with knives.

The zealous Rebirther is also skilled at helping you dredge up all the festering emotional detritus that lurks at the bottom of your life, and that you would prefer to stay there – by just getting you to breathe a lot.

Strangely though, while she encourages her clients to re-live suffering as much as possible, she herself thrives. She exudes an unnatural air of relentless positivity. She is passionately assured of her own deservingness. And she is extremely skilled at opening people's cans of emotional worms and then disappearing from sight.

The Eco-warrior

The ecological guerrilla loves to live dangerously, in pursuit of his passion to protect his beloved environment against the massed forces of rapacious capitalists, polluting industrialists, corrupt governments and ruthless property developers. Single-handedly if necessary, he will take any risk. He is willing to lie in front of the bulldozer in order to save a threatened meadow. He will engage in stand-offs with baton-wielding police forces to hold up a crazy road-building programme. He will expose himself to the fury of the hunter whose hunt he is sabotaging. He doesn't mind living among the tree-tops for a year or so to save a forest.

He is not averse to using his own body to block a foul-smelling toxic effluent pipe. He's happy about putting himself between the tree and the logger's chainsaw, or between a whale and the Japanese whaling ship that's just about to harpoon it. He thinks nothing of abseiling down the inside of an industrial chimney, scaling razor-wire security fencing, or being attacked with CS gas. He positively relishes the prospect of capturing an Atlantic oil platform, putting a giant tanker out of action, taking out a genetic engineering lab, or infiltrating a nuclear power station during meltdown. He frequently liberates tarantula spiders at his local petshop. The sight of his ex-army camouflage jacket, green-tinted glasses, nose-rings, dread-locks and German technical boots strikes fear into the heart of every security guard on the planet.

However, when this valiant ecological terrorist is off-duty, there's nothing he likes better than to return to his suburban bungalow, give his wife a peck on the cheek, put the kids to bed and read them a nice story, get his feet up with a cup of hot chocolate, and watch a video of *The Sound of Music*.

The Workshop Fanatic

This woman is dedicated to doing at least twice as many transformative workshops as she has spare time for.

She is always to be seen in shapeless designer jogging outfits, usually turquoise; for a window of workshop-opportunity could suddenly open at any moment. She also sports an exaggerated display of big crystals, power bangles, healing amulet, potentized foot jewellery and other enabling personal adornments. And she never goes anywhere without her copy of the *Complete National Guide to Esoteric Workshops, Courses and Trainings*. In her vacation time, she takes holistic holidays abroad for the sheer joy of spending every minute of every day relentlessly pursuing workshop nirvana.

She sees to it that she gets her money's worth at every event she attends. She always occupies the best seat in the front row, listens the most enthusiastically, asks the most questions, steps up the quickest when a volunteer is required, and takes the most notes. She's well known to all the speakers and seminar leaders on the international circuit, whom she has a habit of falling hopelessly in love with and throwing herself at. One or two of the less scrupulous of these chaps will occasionally take her up on the offer. She's done so many stress management programmes that it's seriously damaged her health. But she remains indominably exuberant in her quest.

She's constantly driven on by the urge to find her true self and the ultimate solution to all her problems. She fills her time with so much activity that there just isn't any space left for experiencing emotions, or having anything like a proper relationship. The irony is that her search is so breathlessly frantic that the last thing she's going to get in touch with is her true self.

The Prophet of Gloom

This man has appeared in every culture down through the ages. When the Orville brothers showed him their idea, he said it would never fly. When people first tried to grow crops, he said no good would come of it. When the wheel was invented he said it would mark the end of civilization. He has been the purveyor of Protestant puritanism, Catholic guilt and every variety of Fundamentalist self-flagellation. As he went down with the *Titanic*, his last words were probably, 'I told you so.'

He is usually a lone individual who shoulders the burden of letting everyone know that things are bad and getting worse, that life was never meant to be enjoyed anyway, and that after you die your problems really begin. The contemporary Prophet of Gloom is an inspired visionary driven by wildly pessimistic interpretations of Nostradamus, the Book of Revelations, the Akashic Records and a morbid entity channelled by his Aunt Ethel. Guided by such souls from other dimensions, he warns of devastating catastrophes, about to engulf our entire solar system.

This man is dangerous, and should not be approached. He's more worrying than his kindred spirits of doom – the Heavy Hippie, who picks up bad vibes everywhere he goes, or the Baleful Buddhist, who is deeply steeped in negative karma… The Prophet of Gloom is never content to be miserable on his own; he wants the whole world filled with despair and dread. None of this would be so problematic if we hadn't just realized that our destiny is largely created by what is in our minds. The Prophet of Gloom's mission, then, is to get us all hooked into the self-fulfilling power of creative negative thinking. What a party they'd have had on the *Titanic* if he hadn't been on board.

The Eclectic Oracle

The word 'eclectic' used to signify mastery of a great number of different disciplines; but it now seems to mean not having gone into any of them in any depth at all. Nevertheless, the Eclectic Oracle seems able to make a tidy living, because people are always keen to find intriguing ways of gaining access to the Great Unknown. As far as she is concerned, the more techniques she has up her sleeve the better.

So she can cast the I Ching for you. She can read your Rune stones, tea leaves or coffee grounds. She can consult playing cards, native American medicine cards, Angel cards, or any one of her 27 decks of Tarot. She does good old fashioned scrying with the crystal ball. She knows a bit about dream interpretation. She uses nine different kinds of astrology. She has delved into the ancient Egyptian Book of Thoth, and considers herself a dab hand at the Qabala. She can tell weird things about you by studying the patterns of dirt under your fingernails. She is adept at reading the Mayan Corn Husks, throwing the Mongolian Rhubarb Sticks and deciphering the Celtic Oracle of the Burnt Toast.

Her greatest skill is the ability to make up for lack of in-depth knowledge by improvization. Her most annoying habit is giving unsolicited readings to all and sundry, wherever she is.

One can't help wondering whether all this divination stuff isn't just a subtle way of having a bit more control over people and things. But she means well, bless her heart. And so she carries on, helping one and all whether they want to be helped or not, not being at all put off by being wrong much of the time, and sticking by her trusty motto – if at first you don't succeed: scry, scry and scry again!

The Relationship Addict

This person thinks of himself as an incurable romantic; well, he's certainly right about the incurable bit. He's never been outside of a relationship for more than a couple of days at a time. He thinks he's incredibly good at relationships, because he's had so many of them; it doesn't seem to occur to him that it might be the other way round. Many people see a relationship as an opportunity to challenge their personal issues and to grow; not so the Relationship Addict. Relationship is his opportunity not to deal with stuff; he actually manages to increase the package of suppressed anger, pain, and grief that he carries into each new partnership.

If he meets you in the street he will tell you that his new liaison is what he's always been looking for; he is now deliriously happy; he'll admit that the previous one was fatally flawed. The following week he's in a new one; he has now truly found his soul mate for life, and is ecstatic beyond belief; the last relationship was a sheer living hell. And so it goes on. He avoids being devastated by the ending of these scenarios by not investing too deeply in any of them. Of course, the origins of all this are very much to do with his mother. She loved him too cloyingly, breast fed him too copiously, sent him to college half a block from home, and continues to be a guiding force, from beyond the grave.

Yet this man does have certain positive points. He's very charming, resourceful at meeting new partners, and skilled at hiding his desperation to do so. He has scored at venues as diverse as barefoot boogies, holistic holidays, Buddhist retreats and celibacy workshops; also once at a meeting of Co-dependents Anonymous. Oddly enough, this last led to the longest lasting relationship he's ever had – with someone exactly like himself.